HISTORIC PHOTOS OF
LAKE TAHOE

TEXT AND CAPTIONS BY ELLEN DREWES

TURNER

PUBLISHING COMPANY

The steamer *Meteor* with passengers and crew visible. Launched August 27, 1876, from Glenbrook, the "Greyhound of the Lake" was at that time the largest and fastest inland waterway tug in the country, managing 20 knots and measuring 70 feet in length.

HISTORIC PHOTOS OF
LAKE TAHOE

Turner Publishing Company
www.turnerpublishing.com

Historic Photos of Lake Tahoe

Library of Congress Control Number: 2008901850

ISBN-13: 978-1-59652-447-7

Printed in the United States of America

ISBN 978-1-68442-022-3 (hc)

CONTENTS

Water skiing on Lake Tahoe around the 1950s. From the boat, one woman watches as another skis the lake, with Shakespeare Rock in the background.

Acknowledgments

This volume, *Historic Photos of Lake Tahoe,* is the result of the cooperation and efforts of many individuals, organizations, and corporations. It is with great thanks that we acknowledge the valuable contribution of the following for their generous support:

Library of Congress
Special Collections, the University of Nevada, Reno Library

The author wishes to acknowledge Kathryn Totton, Photo Archivist in Special Collections at the University of Nevada, Reno Libraries, who has researched the background of many of the photographs in this book; Donnelyn Curtis, Head of Special Collections at the University of Nevada, Reno Libraries, who selected several of the photographs; Johanna Raymond and Melissa Rivera, student assistants in Special Collections who digitized the photographs; the many photographers who documented Lake Tahoe's history so beautifully, especially Gus Bundy; and the many donors who lovingly preserved and generously provided the photographs to Special Collections, especially Dr. James Herz and Bethel Van Tassel.

With the exception of touching up imperfections that have accrued with the passage of time, rendering color as black-and-white for a few of the later images, and cropping where necessary, no changes have been made to the photographs. The focus and clarity of many images is limited to the technology and the ability of the photographer at the time they were recorded.

PREFACE

"So singularly clear was the water that when it was only twenty or thirty feet deep the bottom was so perfectly distinct that the boat seemed floating in the air! . . . so strong was the sense of floating high aloft in mid-nothingness, that we called these boat excursions 'balloon voyages'" wrote Mark Twain. He was describing his idyllic encounter with Lake Tahoe, the largest alpine lake, one of the highest lakes, and the second deepest lake in the United States.

Crystal-clear Lake Tahoe is geographically unique, straddling California and Nevada and lying on a fault line that can subject it to earthquakes, and potentially tsunamis. Its history began with early inhabitants the Washoe, who made a summer pilgrimage from the Carson Valley to its cooler climes, and continued with explorers John Fremont, Kit Carson, and their party, who first sighted the lake in 1844 from points southwest. When the Comstock silver lode was discovered near Virginia City in 1859, only a short distance east, the Bonanza Road became the first west-to-east road across the mountains, built to accommodate fortune hunters, who were trekking northerly Beckworth Pass and Donner Pass, and Carson Pass to the south, to cash in on the region's mineral wealth. To supply lumber for mines and settlements, a logging campaign sprang up, which stripped the Tahoe area of its rich conifer forests between 1860 and 1890. Dan De Quille, an editor at the *Virginia City Territorial Enterprise,* wrote, "The Comstock Lode may truthfully be said to be the tomb of the forests of the Sierras. Millions on millions of feet of lumber are annually buried in the mines, nevermore to be resurrected."

Mark Twain was not alone in his appreciation for the area's natural beauty. Other early visitors included George Wharton James, who wrote the rhapsodic *Lake Tahoe: Lake of the Sky* in 1915, and John Muir, whose trips to Yosemite and Lake Tahoe were among the inspirations that led him to found the Sierra Club in 1892 in San Francisco. As mining and logging depleted stores of natural wealth, a bonanza of leisure resorts took its place, catering to well-heeled San Franciscans looking for respite from the city. The Tallac House, Tahoe Tavern, and Glenbrook Inn provided lavish accommodation to visitors, who plied the lake by steamship, took in the area's bucolic vistas, and imbibed the rejuvenating effects of Tahoe's sanguine climate.

Lake Tahoe became one of the first areas to benefit from early efforts at environmental protection as local community leaders led efforts to replant forests and promote the natural beauty of the region as a national treasure. Efforts in 1912, 1913, and 1918 to designate the basin a national park, however, were unsuccessful. By automobile, Americans came in added numbers in the 1920s, which led to the building and paving of more roads, which led in turn to the building of more lodges and retreats. After the legalization of gambling in Nevada in 1931, casinos began springing up all over Tahoe's lakeside resort community on the Nevada side. Harvey's Wagon Wheel Saloon and Gambling Hall and the Cal-Neva Resort on the North Shore—once owned by Frank Sinatra—were among the many popular venues.

Following World War II, Tahoe experienced a building boom and upsurge in population, and with the coming of the Squaw Valley Olympics in 1960, the region was placed squarely on the map. The number of permanent residents increased from 10,000 to 50,000, and summer residents from 10,000 to 90,000, over the next 20 years. From 1968 forward, as fear that the famous transparency of the lake's waters—with visibility to 75 feet in places—could be lost, concern for the protection of the Tahoe ecosystem began to dominate local policy. In the 1980s, development slowed after controls were placed on land use.

Today, the sparkling waters and treasured history of Lake Tahoe are a reminder of the broader narratives that have shaped and continue to shape the American West. The Tahoe area is host annually to millions of visitors, who come to ski and snow tube, hike the 165-mile Tahoe Rim Trail that circumnavigates the lake, relax at the lodges, try their luck at the casinos, or retreat to the serenity and repose afforded by the many area parks.

Checklist of Lake Tahoe Facts

•Tahoe is 22 miles long, 12 miles wide, has 72 miles of shoreline, and covers 191 square miles of surface area.
•Tallest area peaks are Freel Peak, at 10,881 feet; Monument Peak, at 10,067 feet; Pyramid Peak, at 9,983 feet; and Mount Tallac, at 9,735 feet—all composed of granite.
•Mount Pluto on the north is an extinct volcano that once created a natural dam for the lake.
•Tahoe is fed by 63 streams, but only the Lower Truckee River flows out, emptying into Pyramid Lake to the north.
• The Indian for Tahoe, "Da-ow-a-ga," means "big water."
•Nestled at 6,229 feet above sea level between two peaks of the Sierra Nevada, Lake Tahoe has been measured at 1,645 feet at Crystal Bay, its deepest point.
•Average annual precipitation is 30 inches, including 216 inches of snow and 8.3 inches of rainfall.
•Lake volume is 39 trillion gallons and 700 years would be required to refill the lake if it were drained.

•The lake never freezes because the waters are always in motion. At a depth of 600 feet, the waters are 39 degrees F year-round. At the surface, temperatures reach as high as 68 degrees F.
•The area is home to black bear, bald eagles, the yellow-headed blackbird, coyote, mule deer, Indian paintbrush, dwarf alpine aster, alder, aspen, and many other flora and fauna.
•Fannette Island is the lake's only island.
•The Ponderosa Ranch of TV's *Bonanza* is located on the Nevada side of the lake, as was the Corleone compound in *The Godfather: Part II*.
•The top 6 feet of the lake, used as a reservoir, are controlled by a dam on the Tahoe City end.
•Mark Twain accidentally started a forest fire here, according to chapter XXIII of his picaresque classic *Roughing It*.

A freight wagon and team of horses in the Sierra Nevada around 1860. After the discovery of gold in California in 1849, trails across the Sierra Nevada became crowded with California-bound freight wagons and would-be miners who chose to brave the treacherous mountains rather than alternate routes around Cape Horn or across the Isthmus of Panama. Between twenty and thirty thousand gold-seekers crossed the mountains north or south of Lake Tahoe.

EARLY DAYS AND PIONEER WAYS

(1860–1900)

Nestled between two peaks of the Sierra Nevada and over 6,200 feet above sea level, breathtaking Lake Tahoe had been the sacred summer home for millennia to Washoe Indians when John Fremont and Kit Carson stumbled across it in 1844. The party was mapping the Oregon Trail and looking for the mythical "Buenaventura River," which had been described by early geographers as flowing into the Gulf of Mexico or San Francisco Bay. Instead, they found the lake.

The largest alpine lake in North America, crystal-clear Lake Tahoe's geographic location established its destiny as a backdrop to the stories and struggles that defined the American West. Soon after Fremont's discovery, pioneers began to follow his route across the Sierra on their way to start new lives in Oregon and California. Among them was the ill-fated Donner party, which became stranded in the Sierra Nevada when a snowstorm blocked their progress. Over a series of grim months, the stranded travelers ran out of food and resorted to cannibalism. Of the original 87, 47 of the party survived to complete the journey.

Three years later, gold was discovered in California and routes over the Sierra became crowded with an onslaught of fortune-seeking forty-niners. When silver was discovered near Virginia City in 1859, the first west-to-east road across the mountains, the "Bonanza Road," was built for fortune hunters eager to cash in on the massive Comstock Lode. Among the early visitors to the area was Mark Twain, who wrote of Lake Tahoe in *Roughing It:* "It must surely be the fairest picture the whole earth affords."

Silver mining brought a steady stream of travelers through the Tahoe basin—and created a steady demand for lumber to provide fuel and building supplies for Virginia City and the intricate honeycombs of its underground mines. Between 1860 and 1890, Tahoe's forests were nearly stripped of trees.

By the time the Comstock finally fizzled, Tahoe had begun to attract a different kind of visitor—those seeking pleasure and relaxation. Hotels built to accommodate teamsters and fortune-seekers were replaced with lavish resorts for tourists from Reno and San Francisco. When the transcontinental railroad was built, traveling to the lake became more convenient than ever, and soon vacationers began flocking to the area.

Washoe Indians. For thousands of years, the Washoe and other native peoples spent summers at the lake, establishing traditional campsites where they settled and held ceremonies during the warmer months of the year.

Freight wagons and teams on the road around Cave Rock at Lake Tahoe. Traffic brought by the gold rush led to the creation of new, well-maintained roads through the Sierra, often built privately and funded with tolls. The Johnson Cut-off, seen here, carried mail and supplies around the south end of the lake to what is now the Carson Valley.

Yank's Station, from the East. In 1859, silver was discovered 40 miles east of Lake Tahoe—Virginia City's famous "Comstock Lode." The discovery brought a new rush of miners over the Sierra from California, and hotels, roadhouses, saloons, and trading posts sprang up to accommodate them. By 1865, the area around the lake boasted 10 to 15 hotels, public houses, and way stations; many offered beds, food, and gambling while nearby saloons provided liquor, women, and company.

A sawmill. The silver strike of 1859 created a huge demand for timber to build Virginia City and the Comstock Lode mines. The Tahoe Basin had an abundant supply of colossal pine and fir trees, and soon a lumber harvest began. The first sawmill, powered by a 35-foot water wheel, was built on the eastern shore of the lake in 1861; the lumber was transported to Virginia City on wagon trains.

Steam engine on the Lake Tahoe Narrow Gauge Railroad, near Glenbrook. The railroad, built by H. M. Yerington and D. W. Bliss, carried timber from Lake Tahoe closer to Virginia City and its mines. The track was eight-and-three-quarters miles long, running from Glenbrook on the Nevada side of the lake to the eastern summit of the Sierra Nevada.

The Lake House, erected from hewn logs in 1860, was the first hotel to be built on the lake's shore. It was located on a less-traveled route along the lake's south shore, and though rumors of a transcontinental railroad that was to be built through Lake Valley never came to fruition, the hotel enjoyed great success before it burned to the ground in 1866.

The Lake House from the Lake. New York writer J. Ross Browne described the hotel in 1860 as "a good-sized shanty" with the worst accommodations on the trail and estimated there to be a crowd of one hundred to three hundred men the night he stayed there. The hotel was a popular stopping place for Comstock Lode–bound miners from California.

Yank's Station, established as a trading post, was purchased by Ephraim "Yank" Clement and his wife, Lydia, in 1859. They turned the stage stop into a 3-story, 14-room hotel with a large barn and corrals. A town sprang up around the popular way station, including several saloons, a farmer's co-op, a blacksmith shop, a general store, and a meat processing plant.

A visit to "Nick of the Woods." The unusual face-shaped knot in a cedar tree located near Yank's Station was a popular attraction for passing travelers.

Friday's Station, Valley of Lake Tahoe. Friday's became a home station for the Pony Express, the first transcontinental mail delivery service to operate continuously year-round. The first Pony Express rider from the east changed horses at the way station on April 3, 1860, greeted by cheers from an assembled crowd.

Locomotive no. 1, the *Tahoe,* on the Lake Tahoe Narrow Gauge Railroad. Demand for a transcontinental railroad connecting California with the rest of the nation was finally met in 1869 with the completion of the Central Pacific Railroad, which passed through Truckee, California. Around the same time, local entrepreneurs looking to expedite delivery of lumber to Virginia City began building narrow-gauge railroads throughout the Tahoe basin.

A Lake Tahoe Narrow Gauge Railroad passing track between Glenbrook and the summit. The position of cars behind the *Tahoe* at left suggests that one or more has derailed. One engineer seems to be attempting to pass and is watching for signals from the rear in the event of trouble.

A train loaded with logs crosses a trestle in the forest. The Comstock silver rush, along with the construction of the Central Pacific Railroad, created a demand on Lake Tahoe's forests that removed nearly all the virgin timber from the basin.

View of Western Summit, from Zephyr Cove. During the latter part of the nineteenth century, Tahoe began to gain popularity as a destination in and of itself rather than as just a stopover on the quest for gold and silver. Hotels began to be built on the east side of the lake that catered to the pleasure traveler.

View from the Logan House, on the eastern shore, facing north.

Taken from the original stereograph, this view shows horseback riders, including a woman riding sidesaddle, near the shore of Fallen Leaf Lake, a three-mile-long lake discovered by J. C. Johnson in 1853. Water from nearby springs was bottled and sold to health-conscious customers in San Francisco and Reno and became very popular during the 1880s.

A group of young women, ready for a day of shooting, near the Tallac House in Glenbrook, Nevada. Known as the most elegant hotel in the area, Lucky Baldwin's Tallac House boasted archery fields, a telegraph office, lawns for croquet, and formal-dress dining rooms. The fellow at right holds a tray of refreshments.

A view of boats on the western shore of Lake Tahoe near Eagle Canyon, from Eckley's Island, Emerald Bay. After 1850, sailboats began to be brought to the lake or built on-site for recreational use.

Zephyr Cove, facing north.

Tallac Mountain, Fallen Leaf Lake. The lake's discovery was credited to
John "Cock-Eye" Johnson, a local colonel who set off to find a more
direct route across the Sierra. He was said to have named the lake after
his guide, a Delaware Indian named Falling Leaf.

Men and boys pose on a log at Fallen Leaf Lake for this carefully composed image.

McKinney's Landing, located on the west shore north of Sugar Pine Point, was built in 1863 to cater to outdoorsmen wanting to hunt, camp, and fish in the wilderness and experience the rugged "mountain man" life-style. By 1875, the rustic hunting lodge had expanded to include a clubhouse, bar, boat house, and pier to accommodate steamers.

A man and woman stand beside the shore of Lake Tahoe, near Tahoe City on the northwest shore. Tahoe City grew up around the Tahoe City Hotel during the 1860s and was dependent in its early days on water transportation and one rough trail through a canyon to Truckee, 50 miles away. The grand opening of the remodeled hotel was celebrated with a cruise around the lake on the new steamer *Governor Blasdel*.

A boy fishing on the shore of Cascade Lake. Joseph Le Conte, a founder of the Sierra Club, wrote in 1870 while camped at South Shore, "Of all the places I have yet seen, this one I could enjoy the longest and love the most."

An eight-passenger station wagon. The initials W. D. K. stood for William D. Keyser.

Men at work on a log boom on Lake Tahoe, with a small steamer in the background and a dog on the shore in the foreground. Logs were deposited in the lake through flumes and towed by steam barges to Glenbrook for processing.

The Grand Central Hotel, Tahoe City. In 1870, two years after the Truckee station of the Central Pacific Railroad opened, the Tahoe City Hotel was remodeled and named the Grand Central. The hotel's posh dining room could accommodate up to 150 visitors and soon was regularly filled to capacity.

Outside the Tallac Hotel, where hotel guests and possibly hotel staff pose for a group portrait. The popular, expensive hotel offered amenities such as velvet drapes, and entertained guests with hikes in the surrounding wilderness, picnics, horseback rides, and fishing trips, among other activities.

Freight wagons and teams in the Sierra Nevada. When the California legislature failed to approve funding for a road across the mountains that would connect California with the east, local investors quickly constructed a series of toll roads through the lake valley to accommodate those heading to the mines. Travelers passing through the valley might have to pay up to 10 different tolls in order to complete their journey. Toll roads were a far cry from the treacherous route that doomed the Donner Party, but the passage was still hazardous.

A wagon train in the Tahoe area makes a rest stop on its way through the Sierra.

Freight wagons and teams at a way station near Glenbrook, Nevada. Glenbrook, on the eastern shore of the lake, became a center of operations for the region's booming lumber trade.

People pose in front of a log cabin resort near Lake Tahoe, probably Rubicon Springs. Locals claimed that carbonated water taken from the springs was "better than whiskey," but there was no way other than mule train to transport it down the mountain until 1886, when Mrs. Phillips Clark bought the land, opened a 16-room hotel and health spa, and persuaded the county to build the Rubicon Road. The hotel was popular, owing in part to Mrs. Clark's reputation as "best cook in the Sierra."

The lake steamer *Tod Goodwin* at a Lake Tahoe pier with passengers and crew. Steamboats first plied the lake for use in logging operations and freight delivery. As the Comstock played out and the lake became more of a tourist destination, they gained increasing popularity as a means of transportation for visitors to resorts around the lake.

Truckee, located 12 miles northwest of the lake's northern shore, was the nearest stop on the Central Pacific Railroad. Though it bypassed the Tahoe basin, the coming of the transcontinental railroad in 1869 provided easy access to the lake and forever established tourism as an industry there.

A group of picnickers on the beach at Lake Tahoe. As the nineteenth century progressed, more of the lake's visitors came seeking pleasure rather than riches. Wealthy mine tycoons from Virginia City, escaping the heat and noise of the mining boomtown, flooded elegant hotels along the lake's shores during the summer. Posh resorts and the new railroad would later attract more visitors from San Francisco and farther away.

Billy Merrill, Maggie Merrill, Minnie George, One Arm George, photographed at a camp in Lake Tahoe. Many Washoe Indians took jobs working for settlers as laborers, miners, or domestics, often for room and board only and little or no pay.

Visitors stand on a hillside overlooking Lake Tahoe, with piers on the lake visible in the distance. Hiking and skiing in the mountains were popular activities. To help people explore, enjoy, and protect the Sierra Nevada wilderness, naturalist John Muir founded the Sierra Club in 1892.

The lake steamer *Governor Stanford*, a U.S. Mail boat, and a smaller steamer near the shores of Lake Tahoe. The *Governor Stanford* was built as the silver rush wound down and sailed the lake for only 10 years.

A steamer unloads passengers at a pier.

An early lakeside resort, probably McKinney's.

A view of Glenbrook from Shakespeare Cliff. Glenbrook's growth coincided with that of the logging industry, and during its height four sawmills were in constant operation around the settlement. In this view, hills that were once thickly forested show a sparse supply of trees.

The spring house at Rubicon Springs.

Travelers in a wide-runner sleigh climb from Carson City, Nevada, to Lake Tahoe. The horses were harnessed tandem and, after 1910, sometimes in snowshoes.

From Silver Lodes to Golden Lodges

(1901–1920)

By the turn of the century, Lake Tahoe had become a popular haven for the nation's elite. Fabulous resorts offered every kind of comfort and amusement, set against the stunning background of one of the world's natural wonders.

Wealthy guests rode the train from San Francisco and Reno to Truckee, where they transferred to the miniature narrow-gauge Lake Tahoe Railway for an exciting 16-mile trip to the lake. Once arrived, they could stay at the Tahoe Tavern or board a steamer headed for Tallac House, the Glenbrook Inn, or another of the region's many fabulous resorts. Many hotels offered amenities such as bowling alleys, croquet lawns, ballrooms, swimming pools, casinos, and fine dining halls; guests also enjoyed rustic pleasures such as hunting, fishing, hiking, and horseback riding.

Tahoe's gilded age was also the heyday of its luxury steamers, which were used to transport mail, supplies, and visitors to communities along the lake's shore that were not yet connected by roads. Guests attended parties aboard lavish steamers like the *Tahoe,* which featured moroccan leather lounge chairs, marble lavatories with hot and cold running water, and a teak and mahogany deckhouse.

Visitors included celebrities, among them Henry Ford, Thomas Edison, and Ulysses S. Grant, day trippers from Reno, mining magnates from Virginia City, well-heeled families from San Francisco, and invalids seeking cures at some of the region's many health spas and mineral springs. Many fell in love with the lake and began to build summer retreats and permanent residences along its shores.

Efforts to preserve the lake's environment and restore its depleted forests began to gain momentum during this era. During the 1912, 1913, and 1918 congressional sessions, campaigns to have the basin designated a national park were waged but were unsuccessful. Perhaps inspired in part by trips to the lake, John Muir had founded the Sierra Club in San Francisco in 1892, and the organization became active in the region. Today, numerous state parks line the shores and dot the region.

A fisherman gets a strike in front of the Glenbrook Inn. Built in the 1860s, the inn was one of the first luxury hotels on the shores of the lake.

Two women row a boat near a pier leading to the Tahoe Tavern in Tahoe City. Built in 1901 by the Bliss family, the Tahoe Tavern was a first-class metropolitan hotel touted as one of the region's most prestigious watering holes.

Designed to be the lake's showplace, the Tahoe Tavern featured a bowling alley, casino, ballroom, shuffleboard court, and barber shop. Shown here is a part of the casino.

Outside the Glenbrook Inn in Glenbrook, Nevada, including part of the pier, around 1904. According to hotel owners, guests of the Glenbrook included General William T. Sherman and presidents Ulysses S. Grant and Rutherford B. Hayes.

Visitors relax on a beach at the lake with rowboats in the foreground, tents and cabins in the background.

A Washoe man, Billy Merrill, displays a string of fish as the group poses for the camera. Many Washoe Indians continued their ancestral tradition into the early twentieth century of journeying to the lake each summer, where they sold fish and baskets to visitors.

A boardwalk in front of the Tahoe Tavern, where a train approaches in the background and the *Tahoe* plies the waters at left. Duane L. Bliss, the builder of the hotel, built a narrow-gauge railroad between Truckee and Tahoe City to meet Southern Pacific trains and bring travelers back to the lake. Luminaries such as Henry Ford and Thomas Edison were among the visitors. He also built the passenger steamer *Tahoe*, providing what was at the time the most comfortable and reliable way to travel around the lake and ensuring a steady stream of visitors to the Tahoe Tavern.

The Custom House at Tahoe City was a post office and 24-hour waterfront saloon offering two billiards parlors, one reserved for ladies.

The Lake Tahoe Railway and Transportation Company Engine no. 1, the *Glenbrook*, meets the steamer *Tahoe* at the pier in Tahoe City. The *Tahoe* was the grandest ship on the lake, sporting polished brass fittings, a teak and mahogany deckhouse, leather upholstery, a dining hall, a smoking lounge, and marble lavatory fixtures with hot and cold running water. It was designed to accommodate 200 passengers, along with baggage and freight, in luxurious comfort.

The steamer *Nevada* passes Rubicon Point. Owned by Tallac House owner Lucky Baldwin, the *Nevada* could accommodate up to 40 passengers in style and comfort.

Campers scrub their plates and utensils in the waters of the lake early in the twentieth century.

The Carnelian Hot Springs Hotel. Health spas and mineral springs were popular during the nineteenth century, and the Tahoe area provided many natural hot mineral springs. Dr. Bourne's Hygienic Establishment was built at Carnelian Bay in 1871, north of Tahoe City, and later renamed Carnelian Springs Sanatoria, for the semi-precious stones found there. It advertised fresh air, a restful environment, and the healing properties of the mineral springs.

Washoe Indians Maggie and Billy Merrill on a pier at Lake Tahoe in 1909. Billy is holding a fish and fishing equipment. The largest fish on record ever caught on the lake was a Mackinaw lake trout, weighing 37 pounds and 6 ounces.

Tahoe Tavern, to the left, beside Pleasure Wharf. Tahoe Tavern became one of the luxury resorts at the lake notorious for operating illegal casino games.

Automobiles line up in front of the Tahoe Tavern. The hotel promoted motor excursions to the lake and awarded a trophy to the first car of the season to drive over the new, yet still rugged, state highway 40 north of the lake.

Mount Tallac presides over this picturesque meadow, where a herd of horses and a lone individual stand for their photograph.

An old timber dam on the Truckee River, near Tahoe City, around 1902. Early settlers built the dam and bridge across the outlet to control the level of the lake.

Work progresses on the new Truckee River outlet dam around 1912, a cement structure built to replace the older log and dirt dam. Owing to contractual complications, it remained unfinished until the fall of 1913. Today, this dam controls the level of the top six feet of the lake.

Episcopalian bishop George Coolidge Hunting, the third Bishop of Nevada, from 1914 to 1924, stands at an altar in the forest at the Episcopal Camp Galilee.

The convergence of steamship, rail, and automobile transportation to the lake during the early twentieth century helped drive the increase of tourism to the region.

At the Al Tahoe Inn, Sarah Mayo and, possibly, Captain Pete hold a string of fish, with visitors in the background. Washoe baskets, visible in the foreground, are also on display.

Homewood Resort, facing south from Homewood's pier to Upson Bay in the distance, in the summer of 1916. Women and children stroll along the beach. Homewood, like many settlements along the shores of the lake, thrived as a summer resort.

As tourism to Tahoe grew, so did appreciation for the region's natural beauty, marred as it was by decades of clear-cut logging. During the 1912, 1913, and 1918 congressional sessions, legislation for designating the basin as a national park was unsuccessful, but today, numerous state parks line Tahoe's shores and dot the vicinity.

The veranda of the Tahoe Tavern resort.

The three vessels of the Mount Rose snow survey, including the cabin cruiser *Mount Rose*, in a winter harbor at Lake Tahoe. University of Nevada, Reno, Professor James Edward Church devised a system for predicting seasonal water flow from precipitation stored as snow pack and established the nation's first high-altitude meteorological observatory on Mount Rose in 1905. His system is still used throughout the world today.

Snow survey camp on the shore of the lake. A caption accompanying the original photograph
states that "the lake never freezes and, therefore, affords ready transportation by boat to all points
on its shore line of 72 miles."

Some people are born to row. A dinghy from the Mount Rose snow survey rests ashore, surrounded by snow, with a snow survey crew member posing at the oars.

The famed Tallac House, with a combination boat house, saloon, post office, and baggage room to the right. This image is from the Lake Tahoe photographic shoreline survey of 1916–17.

An automobile barge crosses the lake. After the logging wound down, steamships and barges once used for transporting timber carried pleasure seekers to various destinations around the lake.

Men take water-level measurements at a Lake Tahoe site for the photographic shoreline survey commissioned by the U.S. Bureau of Reclamation.

The photographic shoreline survey of 1916 measured the lake level in front of the Tahoe Tavern on the Lake Tahoe Railway and Transportation Company pier. The lake's surface was recorded at 6,231 feet above sea level.

C. O. Valentine recorded this image on August 28, 1917, at Tahoe Tavern Casino, with notes marking changes in lake level. The lake's surface was recorded at 6,229 feet above sea level, the highest for the year.

Glenbrook and Lake Tahoe from the top of Shakespeare Rock, August 3, 1919. A bird's-eye view of piers, wharves, and the vicinity reveals lingering evidence of clear-cutting of bygone years. The hillside holds little or no old-growth timber.

A beachfront dwelling among the pines with views of adjacent hills. The number of private summer homes and year-round residences on the lake grew steadily during the first decades of the twentieth century as the lake gained popularity.

Picnickers on the beach at Lake Tahoe enjoy the vistas.

A National Playground for All

(1921–1940)

During the 1920s and 1930s, Lake Tahoe continued to gain popularity as a summer vacation destination. Roads to and around the lake were created, paved, and improved upon, bringing more and more visitors to the region each year and sparking the growth of smaller, everyday lodges, cabins, and summer camps.

The lake was still popular among the wealthy, however, especially among millionaires, who built extravagant mansions along the lake's shores. Among them were Lora Knight, who constructed the fanciful, Nordic-like "Vikingsholm" on Emerald Bay, and George Whittell, who kept lions and elephants on his vast Thunderbird Lodge estate and reportedly enjoyed a Gatsby-like existence on the lake's shores during the Roaring Twenties.

In 1931, Nevada legalized gambling, launching a new era and bringing even more visitors to the region. The Nevada Club was the first gambling establishment to open on the south side of the lake; it was soon followed by many others including the Cal-Neva, the Ta-Neva-Ho, and the La-Vada. That same year, a paved highway encircling the lake was completed, making it even more accessible to the outside world.

Most casinos were summer establishments, and Lake Tahoe as a winter sports destination was enjoyed mostly by the locals. In time that would change. In 1928, the Granlibakken ski jump, later to be chosen as the site for the 1931 Olympic try-outs, was built near Tahoe City. Hollywood animator Walt Disney opened one of the area's first ski resorts, the Sugar Bowl, in 1938.

Disney wasn't the only Hollywood figure to visit the lake; the area became a popular filming location, especially for movies set in frigid climes. *Indian Love Call,* a 1920s movie about Canadian Mounties starring Jeanette MacDonald and Nelson Eddy, was the first movie to be filmed at Lake Tahoe. Subsequent films have included *The Godfather,* starring Al Pacino and Marlon Brando, and *The Bodyguard,* filmed at Fallen Leaf Lake, starring Kevin Costner and Whitney Houston.

View from above the Brockway Resort at Lake Tahoe, with a steamer at the pier. No roads connected the north and south on the east side of the lake until the second decade of the 1900s, leaving visitors reliant on water transportation. In August 1925, the last section of a highway was completed connecting Glenbrook and Brockway.

Front view of the Brockway Hotel at Brockway, California, as it appeared around the 1920s. The Brockway was built in 1917 on the site of the old Warm Springs Hotel, a health spa that included a 20-foot bathhouse built over natural, warm mineral springs. In 1924, a golf course was added to the area, which today is known as King's Beach.

Pomin's Lodge, built 150 feet from the lake in 1914. New hotels and lodges proliferated around the lake after the turn of the century.

Tahoe Tavern, as it appeared in the 1920s. In 1925, a new $250,000 wing was added along with a bar, coffee shop, sun deck, movie theater, and pleasure pier. Garages for the new wave of automobile travelers were added in 1927, along with tennis courts and a livery stable.

View of the boat house and lake shore at Rubicon Lodge. Famed aviator Charles Lindbergh spent a vacation here in 1928.

Hans Hansen, caretaker of the Newhall estate, with dogs and an automobile dubbed the *Spirit of Lake Tahoe* in 1927. Lake Tahoe attracted wealthy families from San Francisco, who built elaborate summer mansions on the lake's shores, such as the sprawling estate built for the George Newhall family in 1922.

Hans Hansen, the Newhall estate caretaker, is at work cutting wood on the estate in 1925.

A small boat and the pier at the Newhall estate in 1926. In addition to their large estate at Rubicon Bay, the family purchased a second property at Skunk Harbor on the eastern shore of Tahoe, so that they and friends would have a boating destination.

A 1927 winter view of the Drum estate at Lake Tahoe. Hollywood movies set in northern climes were often filmed in Tahoe. The first, *Indian Love Call*, starring Jeanette MacDonald and Nelson Eddy, was set in the Rockies and featured a Canadian Mountie love interest.

The Rubicon Lodge beach.

Winter view of the Tahoe Mercantile Company in Tahoe City.

A group of campers from Camp Chonokis view the waters from the deck of a lake steamer. They are identified as Griz, Dickie, Betty A, Jim, and Bill. Camp Chonokis was established in 1927 by Mabel Winter (later Whitney) and Ethel Pope as a summer and winter camp for girls ages 8 to 18.

A snow-covered Tahoe Tavern. Although skiing and other winter sports did not gain widespread popularity in the basin until after World War II, the Tahoe City Ski Club constructed a ski jump south of town in the 1920s. This area, known as Granlibakken, was the site of U.S. Olympic Committee trials for the 1932 Olympics.

Lake steamer at Camp Chonokis in winter. Because of the lake's great depth—1,645 feet at its deepest point—it does not freeze, making water transportation feasible year-round.

In 1931, a tunnel was blasted through Cave Rock as part of a new highway. The Kingsbury Grade, Spooner Summit, and the Mount Rose highway were all built during the 1920s and 1930s, replacing older, unpaved routes and making visits to the lake easier and more convenient year-round.

Campers and staff from Camp Chonokis at the Brockway, California, swimming pool. Founders Mabel Winter and Ethel Pope believed that girls could benefit from a loosely structured outdoor experience after the more regimented program of their schools. The regular camp session lasted six weeks.

Hazy skies on the Fourth of July. A camper watches the sunset over Lake Tahoe from a beach at Camp Chonokis.

Campers from Camp Chonokis on the shore of a lake in Desolation Valley. The 1928 camp hosted twelve campers, mostly from the San Francisco Bay area, and six counselors. The camp was situated on 20 acres and consisted of a main lodge, shower house, and tent cabins. The fee for the six-week retreat was $275.

Gladys G. Gorman with horses at the riding racks at Camp Chonokis. Horseback riding headed up camp activities, along with drama, hiking, choral music, dancing, and water sports.

Campers from Camp Chonokis in canoes on Lake Tahoe. The camp remained open until 1952, hosting girls from all over the United States.

Camp Chonokis campers prepare a campfire meal at Armstrong's at Emerald Bay.

Hikers and pack animals from Camp Chonokis explore the trail above Echo Lake, south of Lake Tahoe.

Camp Chonokis girls play on a field of snow at Carson Pass in the summer of 1934.

Outside the Bay View Resort near Inspiration Point, Lake Tahoe.

A floating evaporation pan in the river mouth near the outlet of Lake Tahoe was used to measure evaporation from the lake's surface.

Outside the Casino de Paris, on the Nevada side of the lake. In 1931, the Nevada legislature lifted a ban on gambling, which had been set in place in 1910 (though often ignored). Gamblers from California flocked across the state line and casinos began to spring up on the Nevada shores.

By 1920, the once rugged hunting lodge of McKinney's had been transformed by a series of new owners into a modern hotel that could accommodate 200 visitors.

Signs at the entrance to the Cal-Neva Lodge with the lodge in the background. The original Cal-Neva Lake Tahoe Resort Spa Casino quickly became a playground for celebrities and socialites who wanted to escape the public eye.

The Cal-Neva in winter. The original lodge was built in North Lake Tahoe in 1926 by wealthy San Francisco businessman Robert P. Sherman, who used it as a guest house for his friends and real estate clients. It was modeled on Frank Bacon's log cabin in the hit Broadway play *Lightnin'*, set on the California-Nevada state line where would-be divorcees check in. Will Rogers starred in the 1930 film version.

The *Thunderbird,* a motorboat belonging to George Whittell, Jr., on Lake Tahoe.

Dealers and players at blackjack and craps tables inside at the Cal-Neva Lodge. Gambling caught on slowly after its legalization in the midst of the Great Depression; most casinos were open only during the summer.

Cal-Neva Lodge bar, with bartenders and customers.

Cal-Neva Lodge dining room.

The Cal-Neva Lodge at Lake Tahoe as it burns to the ground on May 17, 1937. It was rebuilt in just over 30 days by Norman Biltz and Adler Larson, early North Lake Tahoe pioneers and developers. To complete the new building, 500 men were employed around the clock.

Thunderbird Lodge, the main house on the George Whittell, Jr., estate. In 1938, San Francisco millionaire Whittell bought over 24,000 acres of lakefront and backcountry forest land—most of the Nevada side of the lake—and commissioned prominent Reno architect Frederic DeLongchamps to design a mansion. The estate featured a six-hundred-foot tunnel connecting the mansion with the boat house where Whittell berthed his 55-foot mahogany yacht, *Thunderbird*.

George Whittell in a speedboat. Born into wealth, Whittell resisted a formal education as a teenager, choosing instead to travel with the Barnum and Bailey Circus. During World War I, he served as an ambulance driver and a U.S. Army captain. Several months before Wall Street's Great Crash of 1929, Whittell liquidated $50 million in stocks and moved his fortune from California to Nevada, a state regarded as a tax haven for affluent Americans.

George Whittell's elephant Mingo, which he housed in a stable with lions and other exotic pets.

The steamer *Meteor* on the day it was sunk, April 21, 1939. *Meteor* was the first iron-hulled ship on the lake and the first to be taken out of commission by its owners, who scuttled it, thus ending Tahoe's steamship era.

Harry Johansson's dog team. Born in Uppsala, Sweden, Johansson had extensive backwoods skills. Two months after winning U.S. citizenship in 1934, he was sworn in as Tahoe City's constable. His jurisdiction included more than 200 square miles of rugged terrain, and Harry's dogsled experience provided him access to the far-flung outposts of the district. The dogs, and Harry, had previously been celebrities in locally filmed epics such as *Call of the Wild* (in which Harry stood in for Clark Gable) and *White Fang.*

Bird's-eye view of Lake Tahoe.

The Homemakers
Club at the Skyland
4-H camp on the
Nevada side of the lake
in 1938.

Sunbathers and waders at Incline Village.

Tahoe City, California, showing businesses including the Tahoe Inn. Its ad reads "we specialize in trout dinners."

Cora and Verner Adams are among the guests at Emerald Bay Camp and Hotel on this day at the lake. The bay, a favored destination for boats, was home to many comfortable family resorts.

Globin's Al Tahoe resort at Lake Tahoe. The resort featured popular Big Band entertainers such as Count Basie, Glen Miller, and the Dorseys.

The popular Nevada Club, straddling the border between California and Nevada, would later become Harrah's Lake Club and then Harveys Lake Tahoe.

The La-Vada Lodge, "Where California and Nevada Meet."

Dining at Ta-Neva-Ho.

The Tahoe Inn was sold to the Bechdolt family in 1923 and rebuilt after burning to the ground in 1934. The inn was used as a speakeasy during Prohibition and was said to be a favorite of infamous guests such as gangster "Baby-Face" Nelson.

Two Washoe Indian boys and a dog on the beach at Lake Tahoe.

CLAIM TO FAME

(1941-1980)

After World War II, development at Lake Tahoe began to snowball. Roads were plowed regularly, making permanent residency at the lake more feasible and opening the basin to the winter tourism market. As skiing became more fashionable, Tahoe ski resorts rapidly gained popularity. The 1960 Olympics, held at Squaw Valley, drew international attention to the area and cemented Tahoe's status as one of the prime skiing destinations of the western United States.

By the late 1940s, Tahoe vacation resorts were turning away customers, and new properties were being built daily. Harrah's and other multi-story pleasure palaces were unveiled during the mid-1950s, ushering in the glamorous golden years of Tahoe gaming. In 1960, Frank Sinatra purchased the Cal-Neva Lodge and made it a playground for celebrities like John F. Kennedy, the Rat Pack, and Marilyn Monroe, until his gaming license was revoked three years later for permitting his friend, the underworld figure Sam Giancana, onto the property.

As thousands of new visitors crowded the region each year, communities scrambled to accommodate them, building motels, stores, restaurants, gas stations, and garages. More and more residents made the lake their home year-round.

Skyrocketing development and urgent environmental concerns prompted California and Nevada to form the Tahoe Regional Planning Agency in 1968, an organization to oversee environmentally responsible development in the Basin. The agency still works to manage growth in the area and balance the interests of economic development and protection of the natural environment.

The State Line Country Club casino in the early 1940s.

An infamous hangout of the rich and near-great in the early 1900s, the Tahoe Tavern was the last word in luxury, housing a casino, stage, ballroom, bowling alley, barber shop, and retail shops for its clientele.

The Tahoe Biltmore Hotel on Crystal Bay.

Tahoe City in the 1940s. Before the highway system, the town was best reached by the narrow-gauge railroad connecting the town to the Southern Pacific Railroad in Truckee. The emergence of tourism by automobile drastically altered the local economy—one casualty was the Tahoe Tavern, lost when its real estate went for other purposes.

Ta-Neva-Ho Casino, on the north shore of Lake Tahoe near Crystal Bay. The brainchild of former Buckhorn restaurant owner Johnny Rayburn, the Ta-Neva-Ho housed a bowling alley and the Bucket of Blood Saloon.

Recreational boating, popular by the 1950s, recalled the decades when steamer ships were the most reliable form of transportation around Lake Tahoe. At least three steamers are known to have been scuttled to the depths.

Cal-Vada Lodge.

The Brockway Hotel and Hot Springs were first part of California, then became part of the new state of Nevada, and were finally returned to California as state boundaries were revised. In 1973, the former hotel's rooms began to be sold as "timeshares," the first time the term was used to describe an interval of vacation time purchased from a resort.

A cottage at the Brockway Hotel.

The lobby of the Brockway Hotel.

Guests enjoy one of the hot wells at Brockway Hot Springs on June 12, 1946.

The Glenbrook Inn. By the 1940s, the era of gilded luxury resorts like the Glenbrook was nearing its end. Such storied properties gave way to towering gambling palaces as the century unfolded.

The Tahoe-inspired interior of Ed and Mu LeMaire's house at Twin Cedars, shown here in 1952.

The Sinatra years (1960-63) were the pinnacle for gaming at Tahoe. Frank is shown here enjoying the company of locals backstage. Left to right are Ceta Hooper, Mrs. Tom Hoffman, Frank Sinatra, Harriet Price, and Bethel Van Tassel at the Cal-Neva Lodge.

The Cal-Neva as she was when ol' Blue Eyes first fell in love with her. Sinatra bought the casino in 1960, installed a helicopter pad on the roof, and operated a guest list that included John F. Kennedy, Dean Martin, and Marilyn Monroe. When friend and mafioso Sam Giancana paid a visit, however, the state revoked his gaming license.

A view of the road through Stateline, Nevada, showing restaurants and casinos, automobiles and pedestrians. The emergence of year-round tourism at the lake drove economic development and added permanent residents to lakeside communities.

Recreational boating over the years has contributed to the pollution of the lake, eventually resulting in regulations for motorboats to ensure "clean boating."

A tranquil day of sailboating during the height of the cold war. The Kennedy family used Lake Tahoe, and the Cal-Neva especially, as a Western retreat during this period.

Aerial photograph showing Lake Tahoe above the Carson Valley in Nevada. Federally recognized in 1934, the Washoe tribe once called Lake Tahoe home for half the year. Many were later moved to surrounding areas like the Carson Valley, seen here in the foreground.

The "tree house" of Dr. James A. Church of the University of Nevada, the father of the snow surveys in the Tahoe area.

Scobey's Frisco Band performs on July 25, 1953. Left to right are Jack Buck, unknown, Fred Higuera, Bob Scobey, Clancy Hayes, Burt Bales.

The Cave Rock tunnel road as it looked one winter in the 1950s.

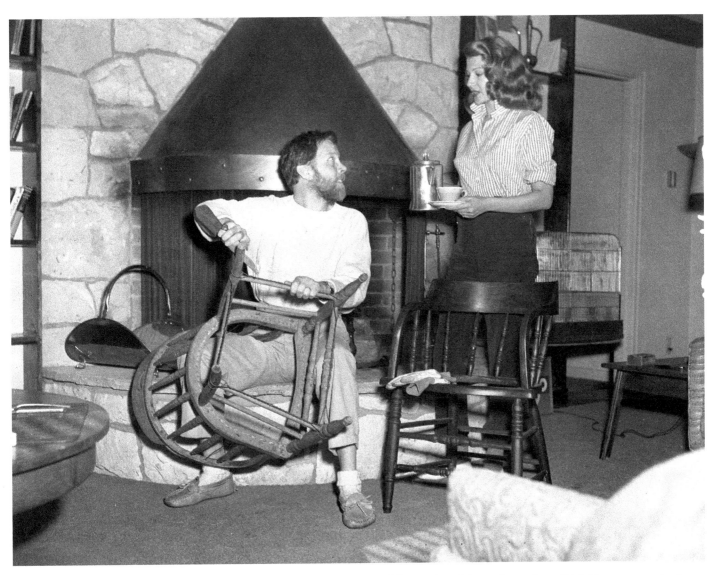

Actress Rita Hayworth and Argentinean singer Dick Haymes, vacationing at
Crystal Bay, Incline Beach.

Harrah's club sign. Bill Harrah purchased George's Gateway Club in early 1955 for half a million dollars and reopened it as Harrah's Lake Club five months later. In 1958, Harrah bought the Stateline Country Club and the Nevada Club on the other side of the street and built the Harrah's Stateline Club.

The Nevada Club, in Stateline, Nevada, was the first club to pioneer gaming at the South End of Lake Tahoe. It was owned and operated by Clyde Beecher and Bud Beecher.

Aerial photograph of Incline Village facing toward the shore from a vantage point above Lake Tahoe. This image comes from the Lake Tahoe Area Council photograph collection.

The stunning majesty of Lake Tahoe has been the source of many fond childhood memories.

Opened by Harvey Gross in 1934, Harvey's Wagon Wheel Resort Hotel-Casino would become the first casino with a wooden boardwalk and would lay claim in the 1950s to having the most slot machines under one roof. In the foreground, Harvey's wife Llewellyn Gross, and daughter, Beverlee G. Ledbetter, take part in a Western Days celebration.

Lake Tahoe informational map. By the 1950s, the lake was ringed with resort communities and permanent residences.

Although water sports increased the recreational appeal of Lake Tahoe, they also brought occasional tragedy. Auxiliary Coast Guard Commander Kenneth Amundson holds up a seat cushion–life preserver from a boat that capsized on the lake. The overturned craft, found four miles off course, was equipped with only two such cushions. The four men in the craft had disappeared.

White Hill ski area. Skiers from Camp Chonokis enjoy a ski slope at White Hill at Spooner's Summit on Highway 50 in the Sierra Nevada. During the 1950s, modern highways made the lake accessible in the winter and led to a surge in popularity for skiing and other winter sports.

Sierra Lodge at Crystal Bay. Winter tourism at Lake Tahoe took off after World War II and the completion of numerous road projects, including Highway 80 and the expansion of U.S. 50 to four lanes.

A winter view of Cecil's Market in Stateline, Nevada.

Stream clean-up effort by the Tahoe Douglas Rotary and Boy Scouts. Ecology projects gained popularity during the twentieth century. This photo comes from the Lake Tahoe Area Council, a private, nonpolitical, and nonprofit organization dedicated to the preservation and orderly development of the Lake Tahoe Basin. The organization sought cooperation between private landowners and governmental agencies to solve basin-wide problems of planning, land use, park and recreation development, pollution control, and soil conservation.

Girl in a kayak. Despite centuries of logging and development, the lake retains much of the clarity that Mark Twain marveled at during the 1860s. One of Lake Tahoe's claims to fame has been the clarity of the waters. The fight against pollutants that feed algae, which creates murk, has generated the slogan "Keep Tahoe Blue." This is one of several images in this book by noted photographer Gus Bundy.

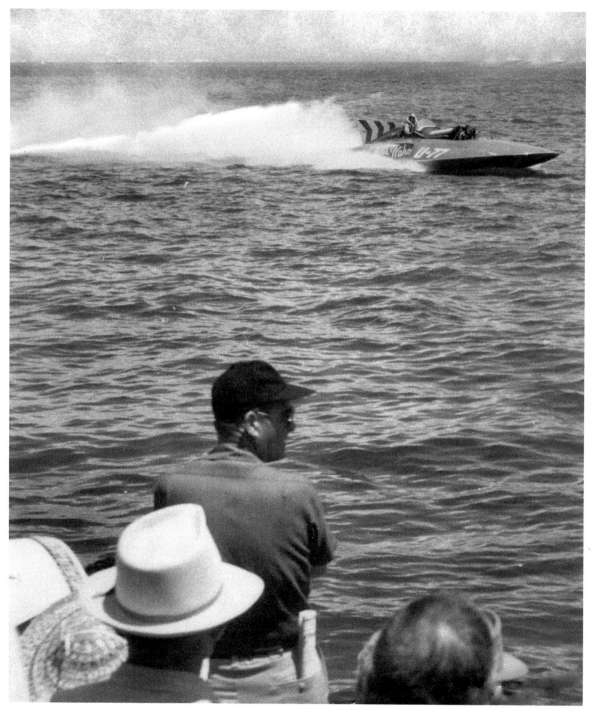

Lake Tahoe was the venue of the American Power Boat Association's Gold Cup race multiple times during the 1950s. In this view, *Miss Wahoo* races past spectators.

In this image, *Miss Thriftway* gears up for the big event.

The *Miss Seattle*, just before she sank.

Down but not out. *Miss Seattle* is underwater as her driver Chuck Hickling secures a line for a lift. The boat's high speed tore off part of her bottom during the opening heat of the Lake Tahoe hydroplane race.

A crowd on the piers enjoys the boat race.

Hildegaard
Willman's Lake
Tahoe House.

Surveying logging damage on Ward Creek. By the 1950s, most logging operations in the basin had ceased.

Constructing a speed-skating track for the 1960 Winter Olympics at Squaw Valley.

When the Olympics were held in Lake Tahoe's Squaw Valley in 1960, they were the largest Winter Games ever held up to that time, with 34 nations competing in 15 alpine and ski jumping events, 8 speed skiing contests, 3 figure skating competitions, and 28 hockey matches. Making its Olympic debut was women's speed skiing and the men's biathlon, a combination of Nordic skiing and rifle marksmanship.

The 1960 Winter Olympics opening ceremonies, at Squaw Valley. A storm threatened the event, but when the sun made a brief appearance, 2,000 pigeons were released into the air. The ceremonies were orchestrated by Walt Disney and involved 5,000 participants, 1,285 instruments, and 2,645 voices from 52 California and Nevada high school bands and orchestras.

Skiing on the slopes of Squaw Valley. The Olympics cemented Tahoe's status as a skier's destination.

Beach at Skyland Camp.

The third annual North Shore Club Last Chance Invitational
Golf Tournament was held in October 1966.

Incline Beach trailer park at Crystal Bay.

Don Beck, pilot of the Beck-Mahoney *Sorceress,* a racing, staggerwing biplane, flies over Lake Tahoe.

Cycling around Lake Tahoe has become an increasingly popular and environmentally friendly form of recreation over the past 40 years.

In recent decades, Lake Tahoe has been studied as much as it has been photographed. The Desert Research Institute in Reno worked with the National Science Foundation in the summer of 1964 to study water quality, using this boat at Skunk Harbor.

A scuba diver with the Desert Research Institute.

A Desert Research Institute researcher at the lake in 1964.

Jim Kelley's Tahoe Nugget was ravaged by fire in 1980. The property had remained in the Kelley family for more than 30 years.

Waterside activities on a day at the lake. Sunshine at Lake Tahoe's high altitude can be intense and parasols help deflect the ultraviolet rays.

The terrain surrounding Tahoe lies blanketed with snow on a winter day.

Even after the Rat Pack days, Tahoe casinos rivaled Las Vegas' ability to bring in big-name performers. This sign announces performances by Liberace, Harry James, and other celebrities.

The South Shore Room at Harrah's. An audience watches showgirls dance in a chorus line around 1977.

Harrah's Hotel Casino as it appeared in 1977.

Fannette Island at Emerald Bay from the west. The ruins of a teahouse, built by heiress Lora Knight, are still visible on the island.

NOTES ON THE PHOTOGRAPHS

These notes, listed by page number, attempt to include all aspects known of the photographs. Unless otherwise noted, images are from Special Collections, the University of Nevada, Reno Library. Each of the photographs is identified by the page number, photograph's title or description, photographer and collection, archive, and call or box number when applicable. Although every attempt was made to collect all data, in some cases complete data was unavailable due to the age and condition of some of the photographs and records.

HISTORIC PHOTOS OF
LAKE TAHOE

"I thought it must be the fairest picture the whole earth affords," wrote Mark Twain of Lake Tahoe. Countless other visitors have agreed, and since the turn of the century the lake's clear, pure waters and breathtaking natural surroundings have made it a national treasure and an international vacation destination.

As one of the deepest and largest of alpine lakes in the United States and the world, Lake Tahoe is said to be one of the most photographed spots on earth. In the clarity and vivid detail of black-and-white photography, *Historic Photos of Lake Tahoe* showcases nearly 200 images and two centuries of the lake and its surroundings, along with the people, places, and events that have shaped its unique history.

Journey with researcher and writer Ellen Drewes as she visits the remarkable past of this scintillating American hideaway.

Ellen Drewes received her bachelor's degree in journalism from the University of Nevada, Reno, and has worked as a journalist, arts critic, and graphic designer. During her ten years in northern Nevada she loved spending summer weekends on the beach at Lake Tahoe. Drewes currently resides in San Francisco.

WWW.TURNERPUBLISHING.COM

CPSIA information can be obtained
at www.ICGtesting.com
Printed in the USA
BVHW020554140120
569490BV00012B/140/P